My

Anaconda

Don't!

My

a cheeky guide to butts

Anaconda

by Kish Lal

Don't!

illustrations by Iliana Galvez

Hardie Grant

B O O K S

CONTENTS

CONTENTS

I remember the first time someone commented on my butt. I was at school, probably between 14 and 15 years old when a friend ran up behind me screeching, 'I wish I had a cute, small butt like yours!' To be honest, I can't remember a time before this where my body felt like something other than a bag of flesh and bones. The glossy magazines I secretly bought (much to the chagrin of my strict, immigrant parents) brimmed with endless workout tips and tricks to get rid of things, from thighs and tummies, to a slew of other body parts I didn't mind keeping. It's disarming to think that up until only a few years ago, shedding, losing and melting off various limbs had been my default mindset. I never even contemplated appreciating what I had.

Despite having a completely average-sized bum, the world's obsession with rears has forced me to consider my own. I've come to the conclusion that mine is fine, though eventually I would like to love it. Throughout history, many movements, activists, writers, poets, models, singers, rappers and dancers have been leading us to this moment – the simple, yet impossible task of being happy with your bum, whether it's big, small, round, dimpled, plastic, jiggly or completely firm.

Over the course of writing this book, I've learned so much about the humble derrière. Not only is there a painful history that goes all the way back to 1810, but there is also a cultural journey through the Black diaspora, that spans music, pop culture and art, that is often forgotten in lieu of peach emojis. Turns out bums aren't so humble after all.

But before we get into all of that, let's start at the beginning.

Researchers regard the gluteus maximus as the most distinctive of all human features. In one study, anthropologists revealed that running changed the shape and size of our behinds, which played a major role in human evolution. It's also one of the few things that separate humans from apes. (Gorillas have almost non-existent butts, just FYI.) Ultimately, our distinctive butt cheeks give us the strength to walk on two legs rather than four. Not to mention that the size of our asses means that as humans evolved, so did our ability to run with endurance – and the further we could run and the bigger our butts got, the easier it was to evade predators and the longer we survived.

Today, we no longer have to rely on our butts to keep us safe, but they have continued to evolve in other ways. The shape and size of a butt can be determined by things like genetics, how much you love or hate the gym, and your diet, though ultimately they're all different in their own special way.

Escaping messaging about what is good and what is bad at any one time is near impossible, and so is making changes to fit those ideals. From the early 1990s to the mid 2000s it wasn't uncommon to hear people ask, 'Does my butt look big in this?' Just decades later, we're bombarded with advertisements for padded underwear and Brazillian butt lifts.

Trends come and go. Keeping up with them, however, can give anyone whiplash. In a span of decades, advertisements, fashion campaigns and magazines can go from selling one ideal to another, without regard for how that affects the very people they're targetting. Eventually, that standard of beauty begins to warp, confusing everyone. What you see in the mirror contorts as compared to what's in your mind, like a funhouse mirrow that leads you to question whether you're beautiful or not.

For those of us still figuring things out, it's hard to imagine having all the body confidence in the world. Yet, we all know that one person, whether that's your best friend, someone you follow on Instagram or Lizzo, whose self-acceptance and self-love feels as impossible to achieve as the butt shape du jour.

I'm here to tell you something terribly clichéd: it's a journey, not a destination.

No matter where you are in this journey, the people you look up to have been there too. There's something to be said for accepting and celebrating who you are. Not only is it astonishingly freeing but it's also very possible. And it's the first step in destroying ephemeral body ideals that hold everyone hostage.

What I'm hoping you get out of this book is what I ended up with after writing it: a rich understanding of an intricate history, a new playlist of songs to shake my ass to when no one is looking, a debilitating preoccupation with 'gluteal amnesia', an overwhelming appreciation of Black culture and the key to appreciating everything that doesn't fit the norm.

CHAPTER 01

IN LOVE WITH THE SHAPE OF YOU

According to New York plastic surgeon, Matthew Schulman, MD, butts come in five general shapes: round, square, heart-shaped, v-shaped and a-shaped. While it's nice – although kind of weird – to imagine living in a world where butts are all drawn out in these perfectly distinctive shapes, it's also not based in reality. (I can't think of anything stranger than seeing an ass shaped like the letter 'A'.) It's a theory just waiting to be disputed – and I love a challenge.

The best thing about butts – and why we've all been obsessed with them since the beginning of time – is that they are all so different. If I've learned anything from all those magazines I devoted myself to as a teenager, it's that beachy waves are extremely hard to achieve and that quizzes designed to categorise you into a certain shape, type or personality are either insidious or a waste of time. Though it is completely natural for us to want to categorise ourselves into neat little groups, at the best of times, we just want to feel like we belong. But there is a lesson to be learned from constructs and fluidity – rules are made to be broken.

So it's high time that someone came in and tweaked Dr. Schulman's guide to butts, for all of us who have craned our necks to stare at our derriéres in the mirror only to wonder which letter in the alphabet it resembles.

Most butts are ROUND

I'm going to go out on a limb and say that the very butt you're sitting on now falls into this category. For the most part, it doesn't have any sharp edges or corners, and words you would use to describe it are soft, squishy and, most of all, muscly. Even though most butts are round, many idiosyncrasies make them unique and special.

Other bums are PERKY

Whether it's big, round, flat, oblong or resembles a trapezoid, perky butts can come in all shapes and sizes. Athletes, as well as those with a penchant for squats, donkey kicks and dance, tend to have pert little derriéres. But don't be fooled – heading to the gym for hours isn't the only reason people have perky butts.

Lots are BIG 'N' BOUNCY

For those of us in the know, it's hard to remember a time when big asses weren't the ideal. Voluptuous body shapes have been around since the dawn of time, so mainstream big-butt worship is long overdue.

Then there are SMALL BEHINDS

Good things come in small packages. Somewhere along the way we got lost and forgot to appreciate the tiniest butts. Brevity is a skill and these butts have mastered it.

There are even APPLE-SHAPED asses

The first time I really thought about apple butts was probably the third or fourth time I heard 'Low' by Flo Rida. Through autotune, T-Pain led me down a small internet spiral where I discovered that another rapper, Nelly, had created a denim line called Apple Bottoms. Imagine having an entire line of jeans, perfumes and accessories dedicated to an abstract ass shape. Typically these butts are full at both the top and the bottom. It's also an ideal mooning bum.

Some are FLAT

Flat booties matter too. Often when a butt is equal in size from the waist to the hip it can appear flat. But we are all for pancake asses over here. Flat and wide, these butts are magnificent, underrated creatures that deserve to be flaunted all over Instagram.

Keep in mind that your buns are constantly changing. As time goes on things tend to change shape and that means your ass can go from a bubble butt to a cute, small bum in a snap. Years of sitting is enough to change its shape, though, it's nothing to be afraid of. Embrace your bum no matter the shape or size, because all butts are beautiful.

Dimples, pimples and other extraneous bits

Face dimples get a lot better press than the ones on our cheeks. Some people try to squat them away, while others Facetune them out of existence. But just like cellulite and beauty spots, these charming accessories are an added bonus. Who decided smoother was better anyway? Even though 93% of people have cellulite, we're shamed for it. For 100% of people who have an ass, we're often forced to consider it as something we need to change, improve or master. How often do we really stop to wonder why?

The one constant is that ideal body shapes come and go. What is considered ideal isn't decided by a trusted committee, dedicated to our best interests, but sadly we feel compelled to follow them anyway. Beauty standards often contain mixed messages and are designed to make us feel bad. It's a tough realisation to arrive at, unless you remember that those standards mean nothing if we choose to ignore them and embrace ourselves and others. Being happy with the way our lumps and bumps look is no easy feat but the more we realise that we're all different, the closer we get to understanding that we're all in the same boat.

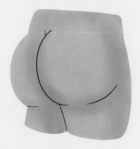

ROUND

PERKY

BIG'N'BOUNCY

SMALL

FLAT

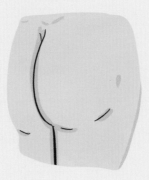

CHAPTER 02

DOES MY BUTT LOOK BIG ENOUGH IN THIS?

If you've gotten this far, then you're probably familiar with the body positivity movement. For those unfamiliar, it's a social movement underscored by the ethos that all human beings, no matter what they look like, should feel good about themselves. It's been adopted by activists, models, influencers, celebrities and civilians across the globe who have collectively challenged the way the media has manipulated our perceptions of beauty.

The old adage that beauty is in the eye of the beholder, fails to account for the bias that the beholder has. It would be remiss not to mention that the benchmark for beauty in Western society has rarely veered from being thin, white and rich. This ideal is otherwise known as the Eurocentric beauty standard. These standards haven't just impacted Western culture, they've penetrated communities all around the world.

On the face of it, holding up a single banner of beauty could seem innocent, until you delve into the hatred it has bred. Today, issues like colourism in Black and other communities of colour are chalked up to lighter skin being regarded as superior because of its proximity to whiteness. Then there's the violence people suffer if they have dark skin, refuse to bend to gender binaries or dare to deviate from the status quo. Many of those who actually come close to achieving this ideal also face low self-esteem, eating disorders, body dysmorphia and poor body image. We're taught to denounce those who are too Black, too fat, disabled, as well as those who are fluid and break the rules because they stray from the standard.

It's impossible to create a joyous meditation on butts without examining the horrors we've overcome and the work still left to do to achieve true body neutrality.

Through campaigns, Instagram posts and hashtags, this grassroots movement has rallied for the breakdown of Eurocentric beauty standards by celebrating people of all sizes, genders, sexualities and ethnicities, whether they're able-bodied or not. It's spilled onto the pages of glossy magazines, propelled plus-size models to success and even seen people with disabilities take to the runway. It's easy to see brands do things like stock broader size ranges and assume that the world is a more accepting place. Superficial gestures does not a revolution make.

Which brings me back to butts. For decades, Eurocentric beauty standards dictated that the smaller and perkier the ass, the better it was, which tormented so many. As a teenager growing up with this ideal, 'Does my butt look big in this?' was like a well-rehearsed hook, chirped to friends, crushes and anyone who would offer the correct answer: 'no'.

Though over the course of the last few years that has shifted significantly. Some may think we have Jennifer Lopez and Kim Kardashian to thank in that regard, since their big behinds were a call to arms for every other big-bootied person to celebrate their own. Suddenly tiny butts were out, leaving us to wonder whether the pendulum had swung too far the other way.

I remember the first time I discovered the Kardashians. At first I was extremely critical of their place in pop culture, but it wasn't long before I was fascinated by a family of women that was able to transform – and even govern – a set of new standards of what being beautiful meant. While I don't look like Kim, or even have a butt that veers from the average size, I felt seen, even excited at the prospect of an evolution. Up until then I had brutalised my self-esteem trying to emulate super-skinny models like Kate Moss to no avail. As complicated and problematic as the family is, and as far as they have veered from the Kardashians I met in 2012, they did help me accept my body for the first time.

However, the ubiquity of big butts – no matter how you paint it – is just a new standard of beauty, implemented to twist and manipulate our body image, distorting what we think is inherently good and what is ultimately bad.

From Kim and J.Lo to Iggy Azalea and Nicki Minaj, the most celebrated asses aren't just big but they're perfectly round, as well as cellulite, blemish and stretch-mark free. Coupled with cinched waists, waif arms and perfectly toned legs, these figures are just as unrealistic as the super-skinny models of the early 1990s and 2000s.

For those of you with thick, juicy bums it probably feels like a great time to be alive. To have your behinds revered by the gatekeepers of beauty and fashion when just decades ago they were abhorred. But it's difficult not to wonder, how long will this last?

Being at the whim of trends is fun when it comes to clothes, hair accessories and even furniture, but applying this to physical features is irreparably harmful. Are we expected to change the size of our noses, feet, eyes and behinds whenever a new it-girl arrives on the scene? Or do we just wallow because the traits that were once considered hot are now so not?

We're seeing the effects of the nascent big-butt revolution unfold before us. For some, the validation that their bodies are, in fact, beautiful is rewarding. Meanwhile, companies selling shapewear, waist trainers, padded panties and butt enhancers have profited from others' insecurities. Not to mention that a report from the American Society of Plastic Surgeons (ASPS), recorded that buttock augmentation with fat grafting has been one of the fastest-growing surgical procedures in recent years.

Though, for many Black people the historical implications of butt appreciation make their joy much more complicated. Seeing white women lauded for their big behinds when Black people have been ridiculed, fetishised and even experienced violence because of theirs makes it impossible to celebrate current societal changes. (More on this in chapter 4.) Needless to say, large bums have been culturally celebrated within Latin and Black diasporas for centuries.

What is and becomes beautiful has a history we can't ignore, and doing so makes us complicit in the harm marginalised people have faced.

So what can we do? Educating ourselves is a great start. Learning the origin of trends and etymology of standards doesn't just make us smarter but gives new meaning to the things we love. It helps develop our critical eye and ascertain when we are, in fact, being sold ideas versus being encouraged to love ourselves for who we are.

Body positivity also has its own roots. Derived from the fat empowerment which began in the late 1960s, body positivity has condensed the message that fat people deserve better treatment into one that is all-encompassing.

The optimist in me hopes that the celebration of big butts is a step in the right direction towards a more accepting world. One that allows people to just be whoever they want to be, no matter the size of their ass.

"

IT'S HARD TO LOVE MYSELF.
IT REALLY IS. THERE ARE SO
MANY CORPORATIONS OUT
THERE THAT ARE TELLING US
THAT WE'RE NOT ENOUGH,
THAT WE HAVE TO BUY THIS
PRODUCT TO FEEL LIKE WE'RE
ENOUGH, BUT WE CAN JUST
LOVE OURSELVES BASED ON
WHO WE ARE.

Laverne Cox

"

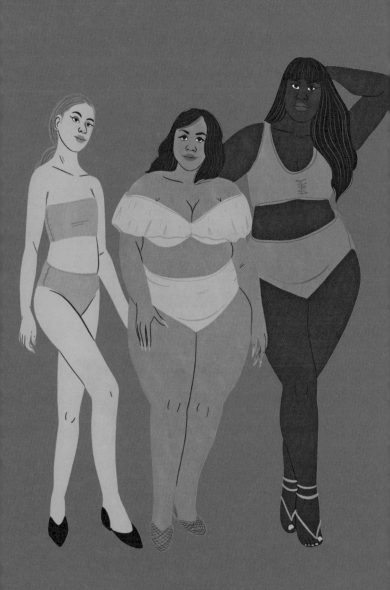

CHAPTER 03

YOUR BIGGEST ASSET

Looking in the mirror, it's easy to get distracted by how your face looks, what your hair is doing and what your outfit looks like, but how much attention do you pay to what's going on in the back?

As someone who used to get dressed with two mirrors, I'm a strong believer in making everything look equally good on both sides, whether that's a cute ponytail accessory, a splash of spray paint on the hind side of a jacket or an incredible pair of jeans that show off your apple bottom.

Since the ass is the star of this book, let's talk about making it the star of your look. There are many ways to frame your bum, and if you picked this book up hoping to take your pert little tush to the next level, you're about to get your money's worth.

Let's talk underwear

What you wear to make your nether regions feel comfortable is totally up to you. Some people love cotton briefs while others prefer a lacy thong. I'm not about to play god and tell people I've never met that their underpant choices are wrong, because I'm still processing why I choose to walk around with a self-inflicted wedgie every day. I'm the first to admit that the only person who's an expert on your butt is you, but when it comes to making your ass look really good, I can help.

In chapter 1 we broke down all the different booty shapes, which will come in handy when picking the right underwear. No butt is created the same, each is as unique as a snowflake. As beautiful a sentiment as that is, it makes it impossible to follow online guides that ask whether your butt is contoured like a heart or a square. Turns out, all you need to really know is where all that juicy fat is deposited – on the bottom, top or to the side. Armed with this vital information, you can expertly decide whether certain boxers or briefs will give you that perfect fit and make your bum the star of the show.

Round

When you look at your bum is it round, like, say, a bubble or a cake? If you see that fat is deposited equally on the top and bottom, your butt is round. You may also notice that your butt is the widest at the centre of the hips, making it more oval in shape, so don't stress if it isn't the perfect circle, because no one's is. Another way to tell if yours is round is if your butt feels distinct from the waistline, rather than smoothly curving from the hips.

The problem: bikini bottoms and briefs can make that round tush look bulky and cause visible panty lines. While there's nothing wrong with showing off your layering skills, sometimes when wearing a fitted dress or pants a person strives for that perfectly impossible, seamless look.

Even if you are pro-panty lines, sometimes the bulkier the brief, the more uncomfortable you'll feel throughout the day.

The solution: turns out, those very on-trend, '90s high-cut silhouettes are going to make life for you and your round bottom a lot easier. Since most of the volume in a round butt is at the centre and the sides are less full, leaving your cheeks uncovered with high cut, low-waisted styles will help even out the proportions and give the illusion of more cushion where you don't have any. Avoid excess fabric, your butt was made for the world of thongs.

Heart-shaped and A-shaped

If you have more volume at the bottom of your butt than the top, giving your hips a distinct rounded edge that tapers smoothly into your behind, then you may have what is commonly referred to as a heart-shaped, or A-shaped bum. People with these lovely asses might have a pear-shaped figure, fuller thighs and cinched waists.

The problem: since you're blessed with a more bottom-heavy bottom, panties with small leg openings like boy shorts and briefs can bunch up. This isn't just uncomfortable but can cause bulges, and if you've just put on a body-skimming outfit, this is not the energy you deserve from your underwear.

The solution: you don't have to give up on your boy-short dreams in order to achieve seamless panty lines and comfort. Spoiler alert: not all underwear is made equal. You may find sources telling you to give up on briefs and commit your life to bikinis and thongs, but it's also possible to find boy shorts with wider leg holes. So don't let anyone tell you that you can't wear comfy drawers. If you do opt for bikinis and thongs, find them in buttery soft cottons that will make the daily wedgie feasible – I say this from experience.

Upside down triangle-shaped or V-shaped

A V-shaped tush resembles an upside down triangle as more fat is distributed on the top of the cheeks. Having this angular booty means you're also blessed with narrow hips and broad shoulders. Since your butt is a little more narrow towards the bottom, there are a range of options available to give you a comfortable fit.

The problem: your butt is perfect as is, but if you want to give the illusion of a rounder butt you can run into challenges with high-leg, high-waisted thongs. Since they highlight how little volume you have on the sides of your ass, wearing '80s styles could make things look out of proportion. If proportions have never bothered you, wear what your heart desires.

The solution: a narrow butt means hotpants and boy shorts will look amazing on you, and will offer the added volume you desire. If you also have a penchant for embellishments, frills and lace, turn up the heat because all of this will add curves wherever you want them.

Square-shaped

This ass shape has equal width at the top, centre and the bottom, though it tends to look flatter due to a lack of curvature. You probably have this shape if there is a cute little dip between the pelvis and your cheek. Fat is generally deposited in the top and bottom of the booty.

The problem: your hips and outer thighs may have the same width, creating the appearance of a long torso. So if you have issues with finding underwear that makes your butt pop, this could be why.

The solution: if you're trying to give a flatter tush some volume, the good news is that high-rise underwear with bold prints, lace and texture are your new best friends. Monochromatic undies can be cute, but if the option is gorgeous bows and tiny raccoons printed on your ass, the choice is obvious.

What's the deal with shapewear?

Shapewear has been an open secret in Hollywood for decades, though it was the genesis of Spanx that changed everything. In 2000, Sara Blakely created Spanx in her Atlanta apartment, after she was unable to find a pair of pantyhose without seamed toes. At 27, Blakely invested $5000 into research and development. Eventually, she began to test a prototype which was a hit amongst her friends, family and especially her mother.

Today, Spanx is synonymous with shapewear, even though their original toeless stockings remain a fan favourite. Spanx became a worldwide phenomenon thanks to its seamless sculpting abilities. Sure, the Oprah-approved bodysuits, shorts and skirts made people's outfits look better, but they made such a splash because Spanx also made the people who wore them feel incredibly confident.

Not long after their release, celebrities like Gwyneth Paltrow admitted to wearing Spanx, helping to effectively lift the veil of perfection that shrouded Hollywood. Not only was Hollywood's best-kept secret exposed, but thanks to its affordable price tag, shapewear became an easy go-to for people looking to elevate their outfit, smooth out any lines and perk up their butts.

Many imitations of Spanx exist, from the run of the mill department-store knock-offs, to the celebrity-endorsed versions that fill up our Instagram feeds, though few compare to the original.

So what can shapewear do for you and your behind?

Looking for a butt lift?

Maybe you have a butt that could use a little help in certain pairs of pants or a skirt that flattens your rear. In that case, there are dozens of options to lift your cheeks that range from control underwear, shorts, skirts and even full bodysuits.

Trying to enhance what you already have?

Perhaps you have a lot of juice back there but find your clothes don't do it justice. That's a real shame, but there are shapewear offerings that can break through unflattering jeans and dresses that don't want to see you shine. They look a little silly, but shorts with cut-outs where the cheeks are can do amazing things.

Interested in a little extra padding?

Honestly, there is nothing wrong with a tiny pert little booty. As an owner of one, I've embraced all the things that make it good, even though the world constantly assures me that it isn't. If you want to pad yourself out though, go for it! However, if you aren't as talented as the queens on Drag Race, try starting small with some padded shapewear that won't give you a lumpy rear.

To heel or not to heel?

Heels are a gorgeous menace to society. While they are designed to look and make you feel beautiful, they also unleash a ridiculous amount of pain unto the wearer. The first recorded instance of heels being worn by a woman was in the 16th century. Despite all the progress we've made since then, it blows my mind that no one has found a way to make these torture items comfortable.

But I digress, they make your ass look really good. Not only do heels give you an elevated sense of confidence – if you can walk in them – they also help you stand taller and straighter, and help push out your butt.

Pockets are key

If you've recently bought a pair of jeans only to realise you've been scammed because all four pockets are an illusion, you're not alone. In fact, the tighter fitting the jeans are, the more likely you are to get pockets that look functional but can't hold a single thing. For years, I've questioned the point of this, but it turns out there's a higher purpose. And when those pockets are perfectly placed they can make your behind look like a million bucks.

The position of pockets is vital. If you want to make your butt look smaller, you can try larger and deeper pockets. Meanwhile, smaller pockets have the opposite result, making asses look a lot juicier. And if you're trying to get a perkier looking booty, try some jeans with pockets stitched lower than your average pair.

Commit to spandex

Many of you are likely already familiar with spandex, but for those of you who aren't, it's the stretchy, synthetic material known for its outstanding elasticity. Traditionally found in yoga pants and bike shorts – all pieces of clothing that make your butt look fantastic, by the way – spandex is now used in jeans and pleather leggings. Why? Not only does this fibre make garments incredibly comfortable, but it also hugs a wearer's curves. And yes, we're also talking about those two cheeks in the back.

"

I HAVE A LITTLE HALF-ASIAN BUTT, AND THE MORE I WORK OUT, THE MORE I TRY TO GET IT BIGGER, IT'S JUST GOING TO GET FLATTER AND HARDER.

"

"

I HAVE CURVES—I HAVE SLOPES AND VALLEYS, MOUNTAINS AND CRESTS.

"

Amandla Stenberg

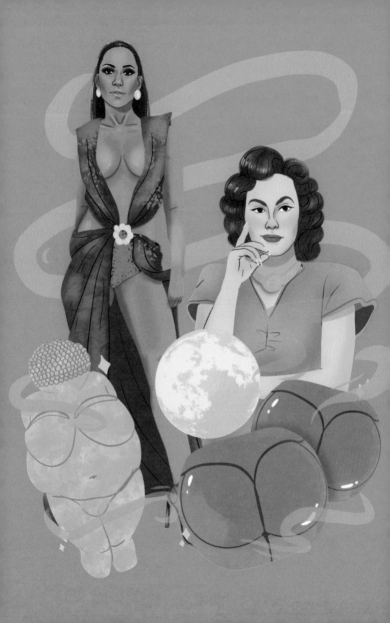

CHAPTER 04

THE HISTORY OF B.C.

(Butt Culture)

While most of us have been around to see the collective consciousness shift from 'Does my bum look big in this?' to 'Does my bum look big *enough* in this?', the history of our obsession with bums stretches further back, at least all the way to 1368.

Society's obsession with butts extends far beyond pop culture and long predates any of our proclivities about the right size or shape. For many of us, it's hard to imagine a time before J.Lo's coronation as the Queen of Ass in 2000, but there's a lot more to bums than meets the eye. Butt culture has a long and rich history, some of which is paved with the pain of Black women, while other parts are underscored with activism, joy and strength. Culturally we've known the derriére to have been the subject of admiration and a symbol of beauty, but there are dark pockets of history where people have used their preconceptions of body ideals against others.

Now crane your neck, turn around and look at your butt. It might not scream 'history lesson' but if those cheeks could talk, they would tell you there's more to butts than the Kardashians.

1368 to 1644

Ancient cake

During the Ming dynasty, when China was ruled by Great Ming, bare bums were already being appreciated. The eroticism of butts was tied to their resemblance to a full moon. Lunar appreciation and moon watching is significant in Chinese culture to this day, and is marked by the Mid-Autumn Festival, which is celebrated on the 15th day of the 8th moon of the lunar calendar.

Mooncakes, which are typically eaten during the festival, also have ties to the Ming Dynasty. A folk tale suggests that messages to overthrow the Mongol rule by Ming revolutionaries were smuggled inside mooncakes, which read 'on the fifteenth day of the eighth lunar month, kill the rulers'.

In 2013 Goods of Desire, a lifestyle store in Hong Kong, created bum-shaped mooncakes for the annual Mid-Autumn Festival. The store offered several cheeky designs including a bunny butt with fishnets and a fluffy tail, a bum with hands barely covering it, a bare bum and what is dubbed the 'builder bum' cake. The cakes, which are typically chewy, flaky or tender, are often filled with lotus-seed paste, sweet-bean paste, jujube paste or mixed nuts.

1789 to 1815

Saartjie Baartman, 'The Hottentot Venus'

Saartjie Baartman was born in 1789 to a Khoikhoi family

in what is now the Eastern Cape of South Africa. Both her mother and father died by the time she was a teenager. Her life was a hardship, with more death entering her life after a Dutch colonist murdered her partner and their baby.

In 1810, at the age of 21 and despite being illiterate, Baartman allegedly signed a contract – which was likely invalid – with English slave ship surgeon, William Dunlop, and her employer, Hendrik Cesars, a free Black man. She was to travel to England to take part in a series of shows, though the details surrounding the deal were murky at best.

After arriving in England, Baartman spent four years performing in stage shows across the UK. Early on, her shows caught the attention of British slave abolitionists who thought the show was indecent and that she was likely performing against her will.

Despite the abolition of the slave trade in the British Empire in 1807, slavery itself wasn't illegal. Her employers were eventually prosecuted for holding Baartman against her will, but they produced a contract to prove her consent. They were never convicted and Baartman even testified for them, saying she was not coerced.

Dubbed the 'Hottentot Venus', Baartman was exhibited on stage because of her pejoratively perceived large buttocks in what was ostensibly a freak show. She had what is now known as steatopygia, a genetic characteristic that results in extremely prominent buttocks.

Later she would be sold again, to a man called Henry Taylor in Paris, who then sold her to an animal trainer with the stage name, S. Reaux.

During this time, she was displayed at parties across Europe, wearing very little clothing, as a form of entertainment for those who lacked familiarity with Black people and their bodies. She was fragmented into body parts, with little regard for her health or wellbeing.

She died at the age of 26, after which she was dissected, with her buttocks, genitalia and brain placed in jars on display at Paris's Museum of Man, where they remained until 1974.

'The complexities of negotiating sexuality in Black woman-hood are usually understood beginning with the genealogy of Sarah [fka Saartjie] Baartman and shape negative cultural constructions of Black sexuality', Sierra J. Austin wrote in Black Girl Genius: Theorizing Girlhood, Identity and Knowl-edge Production.

The history of the white fascination with big behinds is painful, marred with the pain of Saartijie Baartman, a Black woman who was treated as subhuman, only valuable for her sexual traits. Black female bodies have been 'subject to racist notions of sexual deviance and primitivity', abject of humanity.

It was only in 1994, when Nelson Mandela became President of South Africa that he requested the recovery of Baartman's remains. The French government agreed to return them in March 2002. By August, her remains were buried in Hankey, in Eastern Cape province, more than 192 years after Baartman had left for Europe.

1837 to 1901

Victorian spanking

The Victorian era was characterised by a class-based society, a growing economy and sexual repression. But bubbling right underneath this thinly veiled, prudish attitude was an increasing interest in sex, pornography and bums. Dresses that were typical to the Romantic era, which fashioned billowing sleeves, cinched waists and blooming skirts, were taken to the next level, with women using padding and fabric gathered around the back to emphasise their rears.

Victorians were also particularly keen on erotic spanking, with almost 50 per cent of pornography at the time centred around flagellation. In her book, *Pleasure Bound: Victorian Sex Rebels and the New Eroticism*, Deborah Lutz posits that this obsession was rooted in childhood punishment; it was common for private school teachers to dole out lashings across a child's behind in front of their class. Those children grew up to become adults in the Victorian era and no longer saw spanking as a punishment but a 'masochistic eroticism', Lutz writes.

By the 1870s, emphasis on the butt went up a notch with the introduction of the bustle – giving Kim Kardashian a run for her money. These bodacious creations didn't just highlight wearers' behinds but magnified them with swirls of taffeta and ribbons. However, by the 1890s the bustle had been cinched to within an inch of its life, with corsets and tiny waists further spotlighting the derriére.

1900s

30,000 BCE Butt

On 7 August 1908 in Willendorf, a village in Lower Austria located near a town called Krems, the *Venus of Willendorf* figurine was discovered by a worker named either Johann Veran or Josef Veram during an archaeological excavation. The details are a little fuzzy.

Carved out of oolite limestone, the *Venus of Willendorf* is just 11.1 cm tall (4.4 inches), but its proportions inspired global fascination with the tiny figurine. A depiction of a nude woman with exaggerated features including a large behind and breasts, the figurine is said to have represented an Old Stone Age depiction of fertility fetish. Besides experts suggesting it was created in 30,000 BCE, not much else is known about the statuette.

1910s

The Gibson Girls

At the turn of the century, following the discovery of the *Venus of Willendorf* figurine, a new group of it-girls had arrived, just as unknown as the statue, but armed with a new point of view.

Artist Charles Dana Gibson, began drawing his ideal woman for *Life* magazine in 1887. Dubbed the Kardashians of the 1900s, Evelyn, Camille and Irene – the original Gibson Girls – changed the way America saw women. The Gibson Girls were modelled off real women, and they were apolitical, independent, smart as a whip and free-spirited, sometimes drawn enjoying poking men with pins or playing golf in perfectly corsetted outfits.

'Wear a blank expression/ And a monumental curl/ And walk with a bend in your back/ Then they will call you a Gibson Girl', were the words sung by Camille Clifford, the quintessential Gibson Girl.

A cursory Google search for Camille will reveal a slew of stunning black and white photographs. What is most striking is her cinched, hourglass figure which keenly draws attention to her booty. Turns out, Gibson liked to draw women with round behinds.

1920s

The flatter the better

A new group of rebels emerged in the 1920s. Flappers were the antithesis of the brand of femininity lauded the decade prior. Short hair, heavy make-up, bold, embellished dresses and rake thin, flappers indulged in everything a woman was told not to. And this also included rebelling against the voluptuous bodies popularised by the Gibson Girls.

With flat, boyish bodies, bony became the new sexy and this went for flat butts too. Curvier people went as far as flattening their chests and dieting to become as thin as possible and fit the body du jour.

1930s

The Golden Age of Ass

The beginning of the Golden Age of Hollywood welcomed the revival of curvy bodies. Movie stars and singers were celebrated for their hourglass figures and the likes of Billie Holiday, Joan Crawford, Shirley Temple, Janet Gaynor (who starred in the original *A Star Is Born*) and Marie Dressler were sought out and emulated.

The 36-24-36 proportion – a 36 inch bust, 24 inch waist and 36 inch hips – was perpetuated by Hollywood during this time, which touted an hourglass figure and a round, full butt.

Over the course of a few decades women were summoned to bounce their weight up and down, and pharmaceutical companies profited from the whiplash. In advertisements for weight gain pills from the 1930s exclaim, 'you'd never think they once called me skinny', alongside slogans that read, 'skinniness is dangerous'.

1940s

If you don't have it, pad it:

As padding and cinchers proliferated the market, the one name people trusted to help them achieve their hourglass-figure dreams was Frederick's of Hollywood. Frederick's started by providing mail orders to those in search of padded perfection. The man behind the innovative products was Frederick Mellinger, who was known to supply Hollywood with luscious derriéres using the best padding in the biz.

Following the opening of the first Frederick's store in Hollywood in 1947, the company introduced the world's first padded bra. Then in 1948, they revealed the world's first push-up bra, called 'The Rising Star'.

1950s

Frederick's was everyone's little 'Figure Secret'

Frederick's success rolled over into the 1950s, as stars like Marilyn Monroe and Liz Taylor flaunted their unparalleled curvaceous bodies.

'Want to Keep a Figure Secret? No one needs to know that shape is only partly yours!' reads a 1954 advertisement from Frederick's of Hollywood. 'Gives you the perfect uplift for unrivaled curves. Center separation for that natural look.' This was followed by the company's patented 'Miracle Lift Shelf' which promised to lift up the derriére to heights yet unseen.

1960s

The rise of the fat empowerment movement

If the '50s belonged to Marilyn Monroe, then the '60s were all about Twiggy. But before the teenage model arrived in 1965, there was another woman who laid the groundwork for her. Former London model Jean Shrimpton, also known as 'The Shrimp', is often forgotten when it comes to the 'swinging '60s' though she prefers it that way.

Considered to be one of the first supermodels, Shrimpton travelled the world for a decade shooting covers for *Vogue*, *Harper's Bazaar*, *Vanity Fair*, *Time* and *Glamour* – more than any other model in the '60s. Shrimpton quit fashion by the age of 30; she was over the scene, the photographers, the men she dated and the 'dark, troubled' people she met along the way.

Though, a glance at a photo or two of Shrimpton shows that her big eyes, high cheekbones, waif body and soft, elfin features created a new standard of beauty that eschewed those of just a decade prior.

Fashion trends like the miniskirt were in part thanks to Shrimpton. In her mid-20s she was asked to present prizes for the Melbourne Cup in Australia. But during her trip, the model's tailor, Colin Rolfe, realised he didn't have enough material to complete her outfits. So he compromised. All four of her outfits caused a stir as they were cut just above the knee, and the miniskirt was born.

Twiggy arrived in 1965 and doubled down on this look. Notably, she counts Shrimpton as her inspiration. Her blank, wide-eyed stare, short, boyish haircut and long, gangly arms and legs, garnered her titles like 'The Face of 1966' by the *Daily Express*. While globally revered for her beauty, critics did wonder whether her underdeveloped, teenage body promoted an unhealthy ideal for people around the world.

This also coincided with the first wave of the fat empowerment movement. In 1967, 500 people gathered in Central Park in New York City carrying banners that read 'Fat Power', 'Think Fat' and 'Help Cure Emaciation, Take A Fat Girl To Dinner'.

1970s to 1980s

Thinning out

Over the course of the next 20 years, lean bodies continued to be the pinnacle of beauty, though the skinniness that proliferated the '60s would be replaced with a more athletic build. Small butts remained the standard, with celebrities like Farah Fawcett, Goldie Hawn and Olivia Newton-John all sporting super-lean looks and almost non-existent behinds.

But the fat empowerment movement continued in full force. The ideal body shape may have been a thin, toned body, but big butts and fat people were protesting for the right to be celebrated, seen and heard. Together they coined a saying: 'A diet is a cure that doesn't work, for a disease that doesn't exist'.

The Fat Underground, a feminist group, was formed by Sara Alderbaran (nee Fishman) and Judy Freespirit in 1972. The group's stance was that poor body image, and other mental health issues, were being caused by social institutions and the oppressive practices they promoted.

By the end of the '70s, Carole Shaw coined the term BBW, which stands for Big Beautiful Women, in celebration of plus-sized women, fat bodies and big behinds.

1990s

The arrival of Sir Mix-A-Lot

More visible clashes of beauty ideals ensued in the '90s with the golden age of supermodels and the excitement of *Baby Got Back*.

Small booties swarmed the runways thanks to the likes of Kate Moss, Elle Macpherson, Cindy Crawford, Naomi Campbell, Linda Evangelista, Claudia Schiffer and Christy Turlington. These glamazons were neither super skinny, nor curvaceous; they sat firmly in the middle, encompassing the toned bodies celebrated in the '70s and '80s with a new, softer femininity.

Up until now, popular culture had been dictated by Western ideals and big bums had yo-yoed in popularity through the decades. Throughout this time, however, the Black diaspora continued to celebrate curvier body types, bigger butts and fuller figures.

It's no coincidence that the proliferation of Black models, musicians and hip-hop music corresponds with the widespread approval and celebration of rounder, bigger and bouncier derriéres.

In 1992, Sir Mix-A-Lot's *Baby Got Back* was deemed controversial and inappropriate as the hip-hop star seemingly sexualised women's asses, even though the origins of the song are rooted in subverting beauty standards (more on this in chapter 6). MTV even briefly banned the music video, but that didn't stop the song climbing to the top of the charts, where it spent five weeks.

With more Black and Latinx people being given the spotlight than ever before, big butts and small, pert asses found a way to co-exist.

In 1993, RuPaul Charles introduced everyone to *Supermodel of the World,* his debut studio album. Dressed in full drag, the reviews cast a somewhat critical eye over the music rather than Ru, by disparaging the inauthentic disco songs that made up the album. Despite this, the genderfucking, padding and inimitable attitude propelled RuPaul to success, and he later signed a modelling deal with MAC Cosmetics in 1995.

2000s

Diet and pop culture become powerful friends

Progress is rarely linear and despite the excitement of the '90s, the new millennium gave us more anti-butt propaganda in the form of glossy magazine articles, manufactured pop stars, and super-skinny supermodels.

While Britney Spears, Christina Aguilera and Beyoncé dominated pop music, the unbearable thinness of super-models caused an uproar. Tabloid covers were littered with jutting collarbones and hip bones, alongside disparaging reports of celebrities gaining weight. Fat suits – like the one worn by Monica in *Friends* – were the height of comedy, while fat women were only ever cast as the funny sidekick. Diet culture was rampant, from scenes in *Bridget Jones's Diary* to the rapid explosion of diet pills, shakes and remedies.

This was in spite of Jennifer Lopez, who in 2000 caused a worldwide meltdown when she turned up to the Grammys in a green see-through Versace dress, that plunged both in the front and back while hugging her curves in all the right places.

It was a watershed moment that would go on to dictate the state of pop culture we know today, but it took some time to get to where we are.

In 2007, '90s supermodel Tyra Banks came under attack after paparazzi shots of her in a one-piece swimsuit garnered global attention. 'Thigh-ra Banks' read one headline, another 'America's Next Top Waddle'. The horrendous coverage of her alleged weight gain saw Banks herself address the articles on her now-defunct talk show.

'I have something to say to all of you that have something nasty to say about me or other women who are built like me', Banks began. 'Women whose names you know, women whose names you don't, women who've been picked on, women whose husbands put them down, women at work or girls in school. I have one thing to say to you: kiss my fat ass.'

It was a call to arms that struck a chord and replaced the fat-phobic reports with celebrations of Banks's body and her fight against the media. And it wasn't long before other celebrities were sharing their stories.

Around the same time, Paris Hilton's best friend and stylist Kim Kardashian was propelled into the spotlight, when E! signed a reality television deal with the Calabasa resident. *Keeping Up With The Kardashians* started with a bang, following Kim's leaked sex tape. And as the controversy dissipated, the then 27-year-old's large ass became a point of contention. In an interview, she admitted when meeting fans that they often ask to squeeze her tush. 'I sometimes think, "everyone's got a butt, why do you care about mine?"'

In 2009, *Glamour* published a photo of plus-size model Lizzi Miller laughing and smiling without hiding her soft stomach rolls or thick thighs. It was one of the first unretouched, 'relatable' bodies to be seen in the pages of a magazine. This editorial spread encouraged other magazines, brands and advertisements who followed suit. By featuring a range of body types, this proliferation of body diversity injected a lot of energy into the burgeoning movement that had begun back in the '60s.

2010

The Kardashian Khronicles

By the turn of the decade, the Kardashians had gone from Paris Hilton hangers-on to stars in their own right. With several endorsement contracts under her belt, Kim was pop culture's new it-girl, and a Madame Tussauds wax figure, with a scaled to size butt, sealed the deal.

The Kardashians utilised the power of social media with the genesis of Instagram in 2010, and it wasn't long before we were all inundated with bubble butts, belfies and more than we ever needed to see of the royal family of reality tv.

2013

We have to talk about Miley

The 2013 MTV Video Music Awards (VMAs) gave us a pivotal moment in pop culture. In a performance with Robin Thicke, Miley Cyrus – who was itchy to shed her child actor facade leading up to the release of her fourth studio album, *Bangerz* – gyrated and twerked, generating a considerable amount of negative criticism.

It was the first time much of middle America and the world was introduced to twerking. The dance that originated in Atlanta had galvanised Black girls across the world, however, much to the chagrin of the Black community, the dance would be perpetually associated with Cyrus for years following her performance.

2014

My Anaconda Don't

In 2014, the MTV VMAs once again got everyone talking. Following the booty-packed show, where Nicki Minaj performed *Anaconda*, Miley twerked and Beyoncé gifted us a medley extravaganza, *Vogue* announced, 'we're officially in the era of the big booty'. While the magazine may have had the best of intentions, its statement came off incredibly tone-deaf. Effectively ignoring the previous decade of steady movement towards butt appreciation and the proliferation of Black culture, the writer cited Iggy Azalea, the Kardashians and Miley Cyrus's cheeky stunts as inciting the big-butt 'trend', garnering an onslaught of criticism.

'Brava, *Vogue*: Let's just call you Christopher Columbus, because you have planted your flag in something culture's been okay with for some time now – the fact that some people have big butts and other people appreciate them', Alison P. Davis wrote for *The Cut*. 'If you have to cite Miley Cyrus as a reason that being proud of your curvy butt is now acceptable, you're missing the point.'

The general consensus wasn't that big bums were finally 'hot' but that Black and Latinx communities were getting justice by being given a platform to share the celebration of their bodies with their communities. However, *Vogue* and the fashion industry have a history of being reluctant to celebrate bodies that veer from the status quo, and were only now celebrating Black and brown features and customs – like twerking – once white women co-opted them to sell records.

Discussing the proliferation of 'big booties' without even bringing Black women and brown communities (who have historically celebrated curves) into the discussion 'perpetuates the idea that curves are new, trendy, covetable accessories', Carimah Townes wrote for *ThinkProgress*. This dismisses 'women of color whose curves existed long before it was fashionable to have them, and whose bodies have been critiqued throughout history', she adds.

Black journalists, professors and scholars had been having these conversations for years. And now, hundreds of years after Saartjie Baartman's death, the body shape she lost her freedoms over, the buttocks that she was ridiculed for are now the epitome of beauty – but only after white women made it cool.

Which brings us to Kim's 2014 *PAPER* magazine cover. Dubbed the 'Break The Internet' issue, Kardashian posed completely nude throughout the magazine and, in the most iconic image, she balanced a champagne glass on her ass. However, the racial subtext of the photos did not go unnoticed.

Turns out that the man behind the now-infamous spread, renowned French photographer Jean-Paul Goude, has his own controversial history. Kim's cover shot is actually inspired by his 1976 photo, *Carolina Beaumont, New York,* otherwise known as 'The Champagne Incident'. That photograph is from a book titled, *Jungle Fever*; a problematic term coined by white people to describe their fetishisation of Black people.

In the same book, Goude has photos of his then-girlfriend and supermodel, Grace Jones.

'It's hard not to notice that Goude's image distortions have often been used in service of the objectification and eroticization of black women', Erica Schwiegershausen wrote for *The Cut*. In an interview with *People* in 1979, Goude doubled down on his sentiments: 'Blacks are the premise of my work ... I have jungle fever'. The image that appears on the cover of *Jungle Fever* depicts Jones naked, in a cage, surrounded by raw meat (cropped out of the cover photograph, though visible in other versions, is a sign that reads 'DO NOT FEED THE ANIMAL').

The shoot also drew comparisons to Saartjie. 'When I looked at the spread all I saw was a not so subtle reincarnation of Saartjie Baartman – imagery that is steeped in centuries of racism, oppression and misogyny', Blue Telusma wrote for *The Grio*. Ultimately, Kim had the capacity to capitalise on her body in a way that Black women have historically been unable to. In fact, the exploitation of Black women's bodies isn't unique to Saartjie, but can also be seen in video vixens whose bodies gain accolades and sell records but barely receive a liveable wage.

'Are Black women the only women in the world that have prominent rear ends? No,' Kierna Mayo, vice president of digital content for *Ebony* told *The Washington Post*. 'But have Black women's bodies – their rear ends in particular – been fodder for commerce and conversation for hundreds of years in this country? Absolutely.'

The point is the same reason *Vogue* was dragged to hell. White women tend to be celebrated for the same things that Black women do, but the latter are often ignored. This time the flippant recreation of Goude's photos, images that had already caused so much hurt, sent the message that their pain did not matter.

2018

The Instagram Bum

Eight years into the platform's existence, Instagram had become what its creators thought it would be: a place to share holiday snaps, delicious dinners and personal triumphs. What they couldn't have predicted was how the social media app would collectively change societal perceptions of the once humble butt.

'The newest face of diet culture is the Instagram butt', wrote Hanna Brooks Olsen in 2018. Blurred, smoothed and enlarged to perfection, on Instagram your butt can be anything you want it to be, but this has had real-life consequences. A new uptick in gym goers were targetting their glutes with weight training. 'This booty-building trend isn't about health or fitness – it's about selling us stuff', Olsen continued. She contended that the Instagram booty doesn't just demand you have the right proportions, but the best aesthetic, athleisure and gym selfies.

2020

and onwards

Instagram, Snapchat filters and larger than life bums have instilled a new and somehow more complicated ideal than we've ever seen before. Today the benchmark for perfection is augmented by technology, plastic surgery and cosmetic procedures, which have surged.

A report from The American Society of Plastic Surgeons (ASPS) suggested that butt augmentation and fat grafting alone had increased by 19 per cent from the year prior with 24,099 people undergoing surgery in 2018. Comparatively, in 2015 the ASPS reported that around 15,000 people had undergone butt augmentation and fat grafting procedures.

Another trend that has arisen from social media is Snapchat dysmorphia, a term coined by cosmetic doctor, Tijion Esho, founder of the Esho clinics in London and Newcastle. Snapchat dysmorphia describes a person's disconnection of their filtered self from who they are without one. According to 2017 data from the American Academy of Facial Plastic and Reconstructive Surgery (AAFPRS), 55 per cent of plastic surgeons are having patients come to them requesting procedures to look more like filtered versions of themselves – including their asses.

What should we do about the future?

Talking about butts is fun; afterall, it's something we all have in common. But it's worth examining the historical implications and influences behind our new found butt obsession, as much as we'd like to look away.

" WE EVENTUALLY GET USED TO EVERYTHING ... SO PEOPLE JUST GON' HAVE TO GET USED TO MY ASS. "

Lizzo

CHAPTER 05

IT'S FAUX, DUH!

As big butts have become increasingly popular in mainstream culture, the pursuit for the perfect ass has eclipsed working out and eating well. With butt implants, fat grafting and butt augmentation on the rise, are Brazilian Butt Lifts (BBLs) worth the risk?

1890s

Where it all began

The first butt implant happened in 1969. Dr. RJ Bartels pioneered using a 'Cronin-Gerow' silicone breast implant to create volume in the buttocks area. But it was immediately clear that it didn't look the best it could, so the technique was deserted. Meanwhile, breast implants had been around since the 1890s. Back then it was all about paraffin injections – which saw one part vaseline, three parts olive oil being injected into the body – but in over a century, the procedure has consistently evolved and improved, so there was a long way to go before butt augmentation was even close to being perfected.

Just a year later, Dr. Mario Gonzalez-Ulloa made his mark by swapping out the silicone breast implant for a shaped prosthetic to lift the entire bum. It was a small improvement but not particularly stable, so it was back to the drawing board.

1960s

The Brazilian Butt Lift (BBL)

In the '60s, Brazilian plastic surgeon Ivo Pitanguy created a technique that is now one of the most popular butt augmentation procedures: The Brazilian Butt Lift (BBL). However, it would take years of innovations to make the BBL what it is today. He also contributed to the surgical advancement of facelifts, breast augmentations and tummy tucks.

1980s

Slowly butt surely

Meanwhile, Argentinian surgeon Jose Robes discovered that due to the glutes and their multiple layers of muscles, sticking a prosthetic between the skin and gluteus maximus wasn't going to work. Instead, in 1984 he performed a submuscular gluteoplasty, where he placed an implant between the outermost and middle layers of the muscle. There were fewer complications than the previous two surgeries but it was wildly difficult to perform, so that idea got thrown out too.

1980s

Pumping parties

This was around the same time 'pumping parties' began to circulate in queer communities, spanning New York to Washington DC. Pumping parties facilitated underground plastic surgery, namely silicone injections. While many cisgender people have participated, many people in the trans community did this – and still do – to help address gender dysphoria, a conflict between a person's physical gender and the gender with which they identify. By many accounts from the trans community, gender dysphoria is palpable and linked to depression, other mental health issues and even suicide.

At these gatherings, procedures are performed at a fraction of the cost of a licensed surgeon. Trans people, cisgender women and everyone in between line up to be injected with silicone to enhance their butts.

Most reports and details are from accounts of those who have undergone the needle in apartments for as little as $1,200. Pumping is a solution when licensed doctors aren't accessible, whether that's because of discrimination or financial barriers.

However, over time silicone calcifies in the body and migrates elsewhere, which can cause the body to become misshapen, and even lead to hospitalisation. Despite being an underground practice, today pumping parties are an open secret.

1990s

Fat grafting begins

In 1992, the same year that *Baby Got Back* took the world by storm, the first dermal-fat grafts were included in scientific journals, which involved fat removal – or liposuction – from one area to be injected into the buttock to enhance the size and shape. This is how BBLs work, though the initial development of fat grafts had their limitations, forcing many to turn to implants.

2000s

Intramuscular implant

By 2006, with curvier backsides becoming popular once again, Dr. Rafael Vergara came up with a new technique, called intramuscular implants. The technique allowed for implants to be placed closer to the skin but this time with more stability than seen before. Soon, the procedure was highly adopted in Mexico and South America, two areas of the world where large butts have always been revered.

2010s

If you can't grow one, buy one

From 2000 to 2015, butt augmentation had increased by 250 per cent, from 1,356 procedures to 4,767 procedures annually.

In fact, it's estimated that there were 15,000 surgeries with fat grafting from 2014 to 2015.

According to the American Society of Plastic Surgeons, the number of people getting butt implants increased by 18 per cent between 2015 and 2016, while fat grafting procedures jumped by 26 per cent during the same period.

In total, 20,673 butt augmentation procedures were performed in the United States in 2017.

Today

The good, the bad and the deadly

With constant developments in technology, it seems that butt implants, lifts and BBLs are safer than ever before, but there are still risks.

The American Society for Aesthetic Plastic Surgery has documented a 95.6 per cent satisfaction rate for butt-related procedures, though bigger implants pose bigger risks. Then there are side effects, which can range from bleeding, scarring and skin discolouration to fluid accumulation underneath the butt. Your silicone implant can slip and move out of place which can be only fixed with more surgery. Then there are more serious side effects like liver damage and muscle atrophy.

So it makes sense that, because of the hazardous nature of the procedure, it's best to go to a licensed doctor who has a great reputation.

Yet, as more people search for the perfect butt – or feel pressure to have a Kardashian-like derriére – the problem of accessibility comes up again. Cheaper surgeries are available outside of the United States, Canada, the UK, Australia and New Zealand, subsequently causing people to fly overseas for a bargain bubble butt. It's a roll of the dice, as some people come back happier than ever with zero complications, but reports suggest that for many it's costing them their health and others, their lives.

BBL surgeries also have a higher mortality rate than any other cosmetic surgery. According to the American Society of Plastic Surgeons that rate is about one in 3,000.

There have been many stories of women dying in the pursuit of the perfect butt. Each death is as heartbreaking as the last, especially when you consider the lives they could have led if they didn't go ahead with the surgery.

We're taught that beauty is pain from a very early age, but beauty is everywhere and in everything. And sometimes, loving yourself is painful but it also has just as much of a payoff as having the perfect ass.

Whatever choices you make about your beauty and health, we hope you're not risking your lives in order to fit into the ephemeral beauty standards set by the media. And most of all, we look forward to better innovations and safer procedures so that people who go under the knife can come back home.

CHAPTER 06

MY ANACONDA DON'T!

Nothing short of iconoclastic in their lasting legacy, backsides have come to dominate the pop music canon, and without them, the world wouldn't know the joy of 'shaking that ass'.

Most people think that butts made their musical debut with *Shake A Tail Feather,* the 1963 release from The Five Du-Tones. It's a song that's inspired an army of covers from the likes of Ike and Tina Turner, Hanson and even The Cheetah Girls. Despite its legacy, *Shake a Tail Feather* isn't the first ode to the derriére.

In 2014, Amelia Hamrick, a student at the Oklahoma Christian University, caused a stir online when she transcribed and recorded a piece of music that was scrawled across the ass cheeks of a tortured soul depicted in Hieronymus Bosch's painting *The Garden of Earthly Delights.* The artwork is housed in the Museo del Prado in Madrid and dated between 1490 and 1510.

After a brief listen to Amelia's interpretation of the piece, titled *The 500-Year-Old Butt Song from Hell,* it's safe to say it doesn't hold a candle to *Baby Got Back,* but then again, what does?

From 1510 to 1942 booties seemed to take a backseat until the release of *It Must Be Jelly ('Cause Jam Don't Shake Like That)* by Glenn Miller and His Orchestra. It's exactly what you'd expect from a '40s jazz song indirectly about bums – a perfect beat for a foxtrot but dismally prude. The song was written by Brooklyn composer Sunny Skylar, though the phrase itself was co-opted from African American slang. Luckily for us, supermodel of the world, RuPaul reimagined the song in 2013 in the much more literal ass-shaking anthem, *Peanut Butter*. The song also appropriately features New Orleans bounce star Big Freedia, who played a crucial role in the inception of twerking – but more about that in chapter 7.

By the time the 1980s rolled around, the derrière drought was finally over. KC and the Sunshine Band released *(Shake, Shake, Shake) Shake Your Booty* in 1976, sparking an irreverent trend. Just two years later, Queen gave the world *Fat Bottomed Girls* which is underscored by a timeless message: 'Fat bottomed girls You make the rockin' world go 'round'.

Since butts are a muse that comes in all shapes and sizes, it should come as no surprise that songs about them have been celebrated for decades across the globe.

In 1984 the release of the mockumentary *Spinal Tap*, a sobering tale about a rock band that never made it, also gave us an unexpected cult hit. *Big Bottom* may be a parody of *Fat Bottomed Girls*, and a double entendre referencing the group's mammoth bass section, but its inability to commit to the ass anthem is its biggest weakness. Though, the song gave way to other comedic interpretations like Bobby Jimmy and The Critter's *Big Butt*.

After everyone was done having a laugh, genuine bum fans came to the forefront. It began with Too $hort's *Invasion of Flat Booty Bitches*, a scathing review of flat asses from the rapper. It was a new perspective, one that had not yet been heard before. Pop culture has a historically white point of view but with the genesis of hip-hop, music fans were introduced to the Black point of view, one that came from a community that has celebrated curvy bodies and big butts for hundreds of years.

As hip-hop made inroads into the mainstream, Black culture became intertwined with pop culture and subsequently shifted audiences' perspectives. Despite this, it would take some time before we all stopped asking, 'Does my butt look big in this?'

While the '80s is characterised by big hair, new wave music and shoulder pads, in the underground hip-hop and butts were beginning to make their mark. Within five years, 2 Live Crew, E.U., LL Cool J and a Tribe Called Quest had all released their own contemplative pieces on posteriors.

Things came to a head in 1992 with Sir Mix-A-Lot's *Baby Got Back*. The song wasn't just a hit, but a critique of Eurocentric beauty standards – in this case, small butts. During the late '80s and early '90s, the representation of beauty was often thin, white, young and female, but Mix was done with that.

At first glance, the ubiquitous hook – 'My anaconda don't want none unless you got buns, hon' – centres on the male gaze, but the song itself was a creation between the MC and his then-girlfriend, model Amylia Dorsey. As a Black woman working in the industry, Dorsey blamed her curvy proportions for a lack of work. 'It was my experience that he was writing about', she once said. 'The kind of thing that women in my position went through made Mix angry.'

That anger boiled over one day, as the two sat on the couch watching the Super Bowl and an advertisement for Budweiser filled the screen with thin white models and a dog named Spuds McKenzie – who we have no issue with.

'Each one was shaped like a stop sign, with big hair [and] straight-up-and-down bird legs', Mix explained. 'There's nothing wrong with that, but I was so sick of that shit ... I knew for a fact that many artists felt that if they didn't use a skinny model-type woman in their video, then mainstream America would reject the song.'

Despite rebuffing the world's obsession with tiny asses, Mix's song spent five weeks at number 1 and was the second-best-selling single of 1992. In New Zealand (No. 3) and Australia (No. 8) it cracked the top 10 while also making an impact in Canada (No. 89), Germany (No. 25), the Netherlands (No. 31) and Switzerland (No. 39).

Dorsey wasn't just the inspiration for the song, but also voiced what is best described as the 'Becky intro', a soliloquy of sorts surmising the song's thesis. 'God Becky, look at her butt', a blonde white woman voiced by Dorsey in a denim jacket says to her friend. 'It is so big, she looks like one of those rap guys' girlfriends. But, ya know, who understands those rap guys? They only talk to her, because, she looks like a total prostitute, 'kay? I mean, her butt, is just so big, I can't

believe it's just so round, it's like out there. I mean gross, look
... she's just so, Black!'

The second-most iconic scene from the music video comes
immediately after this one, as Mix stands atop cartoonishly
large, golden ass cheeks. A veritable feast of butt puns and
gold lamé-wearing dancers, *Baby Got Back* was the watershed
moment that started it all.

History shows us that it's impossible to discuss the proliferation of butts in music, twerking and how much fun it is
to shake your ass in the club, without examining how Black
culture has, for decades, created and been at the forefront
of this movement. But it was only in the '90s that the world
gave hip-hop and Black artists a platform to share their point
of view.

Between the release of *Baby Got Back* and Nicki Minaj's revival
of it with her single, *Anaconda*, a lot happened.

Cash Money Records rapper, Juvenile, released *Back That Azz
Up* in 1999, a song that became so popular it demanded a
'clean version' called *Back That Thang Up* for radio play.

That same year the release of Sisqó's solo debut album,
Unleash The Dragon, introduced the world to the *Thong Song*.
Months before releasing the track, the then 19-year-old rapper
admitted he had no idea what a thong even was. 'I had never
seen one before', he told Billboard. 'I [remember] first seeing
one and it was like ... you ever seen The Ten Commandments
when Moses went up and his hair was black, and then he
came back down and his hair was all silver? That was literally

the joke I was making with [my] silver hair. [The thong] was stone tablet-ed into my mind.'

But 1999 wasn't done yet. Yasiin Bey (fka Mos Def) released *Ms Fat Booty*; Ricky Martin gave the world *Shake Your Bon Bon*, an electrifying Latin-pop hit; English electronic outfit Groove Armada released their hypnotic club track *I See You Baby*; and the musical debut of Jennifer Lopez was a catalyst in and of itself.

Music has always been leagues ahead of film, fashion and TV when it comes to celebrating body diversity, but even then the industry has had its issues.

J.Lo, a Bronx-born, Puerto Rican woman, quickly became the face of the early 2000s booty revolution. She started making music in the '90s, around the same time the waif supermodel became the new golden standard. Instead of trying to look like Kate Moss or Natasha Poly, J.Lo embraced her body and asked that it also be embraced by designers. She represented a new standard of beauty, especially for the Latinx community and in 1999 was crowned 'Hollywood's Hottest Body' by *Cosmopolitan*.

In 2001 Destiny's Child released *Bootylicious*. The song's most iconic line is its hook: 'I don't think you're ready for this jelly cos my body too bootylicious for ya babe'. Although the trio refrain from ever saying ass, Beyoncé, Kelly and Michelle create an all-encompassing anthem that is equal parts sass, celebration and joy. 'I shake my jelly at every chance When I whip from my hips you slip into a trance I'm hopin' you can handle all this jelly that I have Now let's cut a rug while we shake our—'

Neo soul singer Jill Scott's *The Thickness* takes on a different tone and is instead a rather damning portrayal of how the world has historically treated young, fat, Black women. Inspired by a young girl she saw at a bus stop one day wearing short-shorts with her 'booty cheeks just hanging out', Scott wrote the goosebump-rendering lyrics that are best described as a spoken word salvo. 'That sweet and round, brown, supple bigness, 'cause she so big, won't nobody even try to reach her mind, she's been degraded, exploited, not celebrated, saturated with self-hatred.'

A year later in 2002, Missy Elliott made gibberish cool with *Work It*, a hip-hop hit that served explicit instructions on how to shake your ass. Truth be told, 'ti esrever dna ti pilf, nwod gniht ym tup' isn't gibberish after all but just the rapper vocally reversing 'put my thing down, flip it and reverse it'.

The next few years opened the floodgates to an onslaught of posterior poetry from Marques Houston (*Pop That Booty*), Pitbull (*Culo*), Bubba Sparxxx (*Ms. New Booty*) and Soulja Boy (*Donk*) to the latter half of the 2000s, with Ludacris dropping *How Low* and Lil Jon *Like A Stripper* to round out the decade.

The 2010s enjoyed inspiration from Kim Kardashian's rise to fame as butt songs went from crude to finding a more comfortable position. In 2013 Major Lazer's *Bubble Butt*, a flagrantly fun and ecstatic party anthem, sparked a craze that had everyone whining, twerking on walls and singing the hook: 'bubble butt, bubble, bubble, bubble butt'.

That same year, Miley Cyrus's performance at the MTV Video Music Awards – you know the one – where she twerked and grinded on Robin Thicke during a performance of *We Can't Stop* and *Blurred Lines* caused a stir. Despite the widespread negative criticism, Hannah Montana was crowned as the inventor of twerking.

What ensued was a bit of a mess. Despite Black culture consistently promoting new beauty ideals and body shapes, on her journey to become the new bad girl of hip-hop with her upcoming album, *Bangerz*, Cyrus had not only appropriated a dance move created by Black women, but saw fit to use hip-hop as a temporary costume. Many critics also pointed to the fact that even though her Mike Will Made It-produced album had just a few hip-hop features, she used Black women as props in music videos and appropriated twerking, as well as wearing grills.

Even Miley herself later admitted in 2019 it was a mistake. Though, that wasn't before she denounced hip-hop for its braggadocious and vulgar lyrics. Later she apologised for that, too, after YouTuber Kenya Wilson, uploaded a video calling the pop singer's comments 'racially insensitive'.

'Just watched your video. Thank you for giving me this opportunity to speak up', Cyrus wrote in a comment from her official YouTube account. 'There are decades of inequality that I am aware of, but still have alot [sic] learn about. I can not change what I said at that time, but I can say I am deeply sorry for the disconnect my words caused. Simply said; I f—ed up and I sincerely apologize. I'm committed to using my voice for healing, change, and standing up for what's right. Miley'

But let's go back to 2014 for a moment.

This year, music was as focused on butts and body positivity as ever. Articles still casually propped Cyrus up as the progenitor of twerking, as Meghan Trainor released *All About That Bass* and Nicki Minaj dropped the formidable, *Anaconda*.

Before she dropped the song, in true Minaj fashion, she teased the release with the notorious cover art that inspired thousands of memes. It was virtually unavoidable, as photos of various stars and even cartoon characters were tangled up in the excitement. Even Marge Simpson got the *Anaconda* treatment, as she mimicked Minaj's pose donning a pink thong looking slightly unsure with her ass to the front, smiling coyly.

Owner of AllHipHop.com, Chuck Creekmur, wasn't as excited as most of us were to see Minaj posed proudly on the single cover. He penned an open letter for *Mommy Noire,* writing that her posing in a thong impressed him as a man, but disappointed him as a father, as he worried about the message it sent to his daughter. 'Now, the most popular, current Black female rapper starts overtly pushing her hyper-sexualized image again? Just my luck', he wrote.

Without missing a beat, Minaj responded on Instagram, posting a string of photos of thin white women, wearing thongs, bikinis and all manner of booty-baring ensembles to show that it created none of the uproar hers had, with a caption that was simply: 'Acceptable'. She then reposted her own image with the caption, 'Unacceptable'.

Historically, Black women have been derided for their perceived hypersexuality, just as Saartjie Baartman was as The Hottentot Venus. And the widespread criticism received by Minaj when many white women do the same thing every day without people batting an eye, is the perfect example of the racialised hypocrisy society places on Black artists, even as they try to reclaim agency over their own bodies and butts.

Two weeks after the meme started, Cyrus joined in with two creations. With the first she photoshopped her head on Minaj's body, lightening the colour of her skin to make the illusion as seamless as possible. In the second she used a photo of herself as Hannah Montana and retitled it 'Hannah-Conda'. Minaj wasn't too pleased.

She responded by reposting the first image and wrote, 'Give me one good reason why Miley made this her twitter avi'. When she re-posted Cyrus's HannahConda creation, she captioned it 'No Chill Zone'.

History will tell us that there was no love lost between the two stars, but this signalled the beginning of what would be a thrilling end.

'Cyrus's role in this technological beheading cannot be overstated; as a white female musician who has attempted to 'blacken' and adultify her pristine Disney girl image and then remove her hypersexual image when no longer useful, Cyrus has constructed her career on Black women's bodies – particularly their butts', writes Aria S. Halliday in *Miley, What's Good? Nicki Minaj's Anaconda, Instagram Reproductions, and Viral Memetic Violence*. 'Cyrus's use of Nicki Minaj's Anaconda image illustrates what I call celebrity-to-celebrity scrub-bing, or the use of another's celebrity status to bolster one's own.'

And this happened all before the song was even released.

To describe *Anaconda* as anything but a cultural phenom-enon would be a disservice to the hysteria Minaj created with that song. The video broke the 24-hour streaming record on VEVO by accumulating 19.6 million views the day it was released. I remember the day this came out and how exhilarating it felt to hear an anthem for women who were anything but thin.

'This one is for my bitches with a fat ass in the fucking club', Nicki trills. 'I said, where my fat ass big bitches in the club? Fuck the skinny bitches! Fuck the skinny bitches in the club!' For many people who had never been able to meet the skinny supermodel standard this was the first time they were being recognised in pop culture at this level. But this also turned out to be the song's most controversial line.

Despite celebrating fat Black bodies and bums, Minaj was accused of body shaming. 'The critique geared at "reverse oppression" has, unsurprisingly, originated from white audiences, and the "skinny shaming" critique came from some white feminists', Katariina Kyrola posited in *Music Videos as Black Feminist Thought – From Nicki Minaj's Anaconda to Beyoncé's Formation*.

Kryola also succinctly surmises that Minaj telling these thin and ostensibly white privileged people to 'fuck off' ultimately means this is not a space for them. As Black and fat women have been ignored for so long, giving them space is important and fat butts need uplifting.

Despite Minaj's overwhelming success with *Anaconda* and her subsequent third studio album, *The Pinkprint*, she was overlooked for the top prize of Album of The Year at the 2015 MTV Video Music Awards – which were to be hosted by Cyrus.

Not one to stay quiet, Minaj took to social media to air her grievances. "When the 'other" girls drop a video that breaks records and impacts culture they get that nomination', she tweeted in July 2015 alongside exactly 38 sarcastic smiling emojis. 'If your video celebrates women with very slim bodies, you will be nominated for vid of the year', she added with a second tweet.

'In order to "celebrate" large backsides, it seems, the overwhelmingly white U.S. fashion industry must first attribute the trait to non-black women', Stacia L. Brown laments, pointing to how 2014 was 'officially' dubbed 'the year of the big booty' by Vogue, a publication complicit in enforcing Eurocentric beauty standards, and the reason Amylia Dorsey hated her curves and *Baby Got Back* was written.

'Why does a black butt only look good in white skin?' writer Yomi Adegoke asked in 2014. Adegoke points to the success of Iggy Azalea, Lopez and Miley Cyrus who, by flaunting their assets, have been perpetually celebrated as leaders of a movement, while historically Black women have been shamed for their behinds.

The fact is, when you look back on how derrières have been celebrated in music, Black artists started it all and yet were the last to be celebrated. Instead, their contributions have been erased.

One name that comes to mind is the queen of New Orleans Bounce, Big Freedia, who has not only set the Guinness World Record for most people twerking simultaneously but has released a dizzying number of songs about bums. From *Azz Everywhere* and *Mo Azz* to *Y'all Get Back Now* and her feature on RuPaul's *Peanut Butter*, there aren't enough peach-shaped accolades in the world for Freedia. (More on this in chapter 7.)

And luckily for us, *Anaconda* didn't end pop culture's obsession with butts but rather inspired more artists to continue to create odes to asses.

By the end of 2014, we had Tujamo's *Booty Bounce*, the frenetic Taio Cruz-assisted EDM bop. Meanwhile Minaj refused to take her foot off the gas and doubled down on the ass-themed music with *Truffle Butter*. As the fifth single from *The Pinkprint*, this slow-burning, club-friendly beat featured labelmates Drake and Lil Wayne.

But pop music couldn't ignore the bubbling undercurrent of bum-mania. In 2016, Bruno Mars released *Chunky*, a radio-friendly, funky hit that kept things a little more G-rated. 'She got to shake her little something (shake her little something), ooh throwing that thing from left, right, side-to-side, she got to have her own money (she got her own money), oh yeah, shout out to the girls that pay they rent on time.'

However, with Cardi B around things couldn't stay squeaky clean for too long. The former stripper knows exactly how to do her thing, whether that's taking a belfie that deserves to be hung at the Louvre or twerking. So her 2018 collaboration with rap duo City Girls was the start of something great.

Needless to say, the revelry of *Twerk* is unmatched. It's not just a song that will get you shaking your ass, but the music video is an exuberant manifesto of the artist's work.

As derriéres took over the music industry, one star whose pop career looked all but over decided to make a comeback. In 2019, well into her EDM career, Paris Hilton released *Best Friend's Ass*, her collaboration with Dimitri Vegas and Like Mike. And yes, she's talking about *that* best friend. It's a powdery meditation on being surrounded by fuckboys but unabashedly stanning your best friend because they look so good. Kim Kardashian makes a brief cameo in the music video and seals her position as a pop culture ass icon.

And you can't talk about assess and the music industry without giving Megan Thee Stallion a round of applause. The Houston rapper also happens to be a huge fan of Minaj. In fact, the two teamed up on the remix for *Hot Girl Summer*, an ephemeral summer anthem about having agency in one's body and having fun with it. Since then, Meg has become a prominent figure who not only has strong knees, but has galvanised a movement that returns the agency and power to Black women. Basically she's the antithesis of *Vogue's* 2014 proclamations. And if, for some reason, you think twerking can't spread happiness, then you need to get familiar with Thee Stallion.

Case in point is the Meg-assisted *Big Booty* by Gucci Mane. The glossy hip-hop beat is underscored by booming 808s, while the two rappers play off one another seamlessly. Meg brags about the power of her ass – 'Big old ass is heavy, shake that shit like jelly, put me on your plate and slurp that shit up

like spaghetti, man, I make this shit look easy, I ain't tryin',
I just be me' – while Gucci laments how helpless he is to
'thick hoes'.

Songs like *Big Ole Freak* see the Houston rapper revel in her
beauty and body while the Beyonce-assisted *Savage Remix*
has one of the most iconic lines for anyone with a thick bum
thanks to Queen Bey: 'If you don't jump to put jeans on baby,
you don't feel my pain'.

Despite getting off to a slow start, these songs, lyrics and
music videos have played a vital role in spearheading popular
culture's ideas around body positivity. Who knows where we
would be without *Baby Got Back* ...

Ariana Grande

"

WE LIVE IN A DAY AND AGE WHERE PEOPLE MAKE IT IMPOSSIBLE FOR WOMEN, MEN, ANYONE TO EMBRACE THEMSELVES EXACTLY HOW THEY ARE. DIVERSITY IS SEXY! LOVING YOURSELF IS SEXY! YOU KNOW WHAT IS NOT SEXY? MISOGYNY, OBJECTIFYING, LABELING, COMPARING AND BODY SHAMING!

"

"

I LOVE CREATING SHAPES WITH MY BODY, AND I LOVE NORMALIZING THE DIMPLES IN MY BUTT OR THE LUMPS IN MY THIGHS OR MY BACK FAT OR MY STRETCH MARKS. I LOVE NORMALIZING MY BLACK-ASS ELBOWS. I THINK IT'S BEAUTIFUL.

"

Lizzo

CHAPTER 07

HIPS DON'T LIE

Throughout history and across all cultures, shaking your ass and hips has become synonymous with joy, sexuality, taboos and everything in between. So let's take a trip around the world and discover the vast range of ways to shake that ass.

Twerking

First thing's first, twerking wasn't invented by Miley when she gyrated on Robin Thicke that one time. Though, the origins of the ubiquitous dance are murky.

One source suggests that it all began with the genesis of bounce music in 1985 in Miami, when M.C. A.D.E. sampled German electronic outfit, Kraftwerk's *Trans-Europe Express* and created *Bass Rock Express*. The rolling 808 beat lent itself perfectly to ass-shaking, and that's how twerking was born.

Others suggest that it all began in the New Orleans bounce scene in the '90s. In 1993, DJ Jubilee released *Do the Jubilee All*, where he instructs the crowd to 'twerk baby, twerk baby, twerk, twerk, twerk!'

Not unlike Miami bounce, New Orleans bounce tracks include a relentlessly fast tempo, an infectious call-and-response routine – borrowed from Mardi Gras Indian chants – and a sample of the 'Triggerman' beat: a 1-bar drum loop that comes from *Drag Rap* by The Showboys or a sample of Derek B's *Rock The Beat*. Details aside, it's party music distilled.

Some contend that twerking began much earlier, namely in Atlanta strip clubs. But in *Twerk It: Deconstructing Racial and Gendered Implications of Black Women's Bodies through Representations of Twerking,* author Niamba Baskerville interviews a number of people who attest that twerking has always existed, it just didn't have a name until recently.

In an interview with VIBE, three-time MTV VMA-nominated choreographer, Tanisha Scott, who has worked with Rihanna, Beyoncé and Sean Paul, explained that twerking is part of the Black diaspora. 'There's this thing that people have always come to me with. They're like "okay so you know how to twerk and all this new phenomenon". I'm like actually it's not new because if you think about it, back in the days, and currently right now in Africa, that is the way we move. That's the whole culture and the basis behind that dance.'

The word 'twirk' was first used as a noun in 1820, meaning a twisting, twitching or jerking movement. Over time, twerk – a portmanteau of 'twirk' and 'jerk' – replaced the word, now defined as a verb.

'Twerk' was added to the Oxford dictionary in 2013, defined as 'dance to popular music in a sexually provocative manner involving thrusting hip movements and a low, squatting stance'. Though, it fails to describe that the bum is a big part of this dance.

'It also suggests that the dance is inherently sexual and provocative', Baskerville writes. 'While twerking involves "thrusting hip movements and a low, squatting stance", this does not mean the dance itself is inherently sexual or provocative. This dance form has come to embody hypersexuality in our cultural imagination because of its association with Black female bodies.' Before Cyrus co-opted the dance in 2013, twerking was just booty shaking.

Big Freedia, a pillar of the New Orleans bounce scene, is unequivocally the queen of twerking. 'We don't twerk in New Orleans', she said at the 2014 New Orleans Jazz Festival. 'We shake, wiggle, wobble, werk, bend over, bust over. We do it all. Twerking is just one of the words in our vocabulary. We've been twerking for years, but that's just one of the words in the vocabulary of Bounce.'

Freedia is a gay Black man but everyone uses female pronouns to refer to her. She's also an Aquarius with a heart of gold. Born and raised in New Orleans, Freedia released her first single, *An Ha, Oh Yeah* in 1999. In 2005, when Hurricane Katrina left New Orleans devastated she was forced to evacuate, but returned as soon she could. This is when she started FEMA Fridays, a club night that ostensibly restored the city's joy.

To say that Freedia is synonymous with ass-shaking would be an understatement. Always armed with a team of backup dancers dubbed the 'bootydancers', she has released an abundance of songs about butts that are designed to get your tush moving.

Freedia's music is like a high-octane thrill ride into the centre of New Orleans. Throughout the star's discography are songs like *Azz Everywhere*, a gritty 2010 bounce track, and *Booty-Whop*, a carnal club bop. But then there are outliers like *Play*, which features UK legend Goldie, and interpolates bounce, house and R&B textures as Freedia demands everyone to 'shake your ass and your titties'. In 2019, Freedia was tapped by Dillion Francis and TV Noise for *Bawdy, a* dancehall-flavoured EDM hit. And just as you think you've hit the end of her treasure trove of butt odes, you'll find *Lift Dat Leg Up*, *Rudy The Big Booty Reindeer*, *Make Ya Booty Go*, *Mo Azz*, *Y'Tootsay* and *Walk Wit a Dip*.

And who can forget some of the biggest guest features of her career, on ass-shaking tracks like Beyoncé's *Formation*, Drake's *Nice For What*, Charli XCX's *Shake It* and RuPaul's *Peanut Butter*.

While Freedia's claim to the twerk throne is undisputed, in 2013 she doubled down and led a crowd of 358 people in New York City to shatter the previous Guinness World Record for most people twerking simultaneously. Together, the incredible group twerked for two thrilling minutes.

Mapouka

Mapouka dance, which loosely translates to 'the butt dance', originated in the Ivory Coast. This dance involves shaking one's ass vigorously from side to side, irreverently, as though it's disconnected from the rest of the body. Dancers wiggle their butts without moving their hips in a surprisingly difficult, yet undeniably hypnotic flow.

In the early 1980s, artists from the Ivory Coast tried to bring the dance to the United States, though it didn't make much of an impact. However, by 1998, the dance craze was banned from television and any public performances by the Ivory Coast government. The ban made the dance all the more popular as it spread along the West African Coast, to neighbouring countries like Togo, Niger, Burkina Faso and Benin.

Leumbeul

Then there's the modernisation of 'leumbeul', a traditional dance in Senegal. Over the years, the dance, which involves jerking one's body to a frenzied drum beat, has evolved into something more ass-friendly. Dancers jiggle their behinds to the beat of a drum, sometimes on their own and sometimes with others.

Sandungueo and Perrero

Otherwise known as grinding, sandungueo or perrero is a dance from Puerto Rico inspired by the carnal rhythm of reggaeton. Originated in the 1980s, it's said to have been created by DJ Blass. So how does one Sandungueo? Chances are, you already know. It involves one dancer grinding their butt onto the other and, as you can imagine, is often seen as extremely sexual.

Whining

A regional dance originating in the Caribbean, whining is the graceful gyration of the ass in a rhythmic pattern that relies solely on the waist to give the dance fluid momentum. The dance comes out in all its glory when people dance to the calypso or to a soca rhythm. Some dancers are even able to incorporate a body roll and hip tick into the movements. As a certified expert on having no rhythm, I can say that I'm truly impressed.

Punta

Created by Garifuna, an ethnic group of Indigenous Islanders in Honduras, Punta was brought to the Caribbean shores of Central America in the 18th century. Today the dance is traditional to Guatemala, Nicaragua, Belize, as well as Honduras. It involves two dancers circling one another, while frantically jiggling, wiggling and shimmying their butts, hips, and feet, while keeping their torsos still. While the original dance is associated with ancestral ceremonies, wakes and rituals, today the musical genre of punta rock, which began in the 1970s, has brought the dance into the everyday lives of Central Americans.

Belly dancing

The name 'belly dance' comes from the French term 'danse du ventre', which loosely translates to 'dance of the stomach'. Despite its name, belly dancing has always focused on the shimmying of the hips and ass to, and in spite of, the beat of the song.

Due to its long history in the Middle East, the origins of belly dancing are highly speculative though many believe it comes from dancers in Asia and Spain whose 'quivering thighs' were

interpolated into the dance. The dance itself can be traced as far back as 6,000 years ago, within pagan societies who worshipped feminine deities.

Today, in the Middle East, the dance has three distinct contexts: as a folk dance, a social dance or as performance art. Even as a social dance, when it is performed by anyone, even in ordinary clothing, it is in a much more conservative and traditional way, with women segregated from others.

In Egypt, and specifically Cairo, however, modern Egyptian belly dancing originated from the city's nightclubs and is known for its controlled and precise movements.

The Turkish style of belly dancing is a little looser and more playful. There is a sense of athleticism involved in the dance, with performers using zils, otherwise known as finger cymbals, and energetic movements. Notably, most professional belly dancers in Turkey are of Romani heritage.

Lebanon's iteration of the dance is a mixture of Turkey and Egypt's stylings, though has a fiercely modern edge. Physically, hip rotations and shimmies take the dance to another level and also incorporate doing the splits, along with back bends and kicks.

Pole dancing

We can't talk about butts without discussing the rich history of pole dancing.

Like most dances, there are several potential origins. Some say its roots are in an African tribal dance, which sees women use large wooden poles in a dance for their potential partners; it represented fertility leading up to one's marriage. While others point to the Maypole dance, a pagan ritual where women hold ribbons connected to a pole and dance in a circle to celebrate fertility. Another source suggests pole dancing is derived from a more than 800-year-old Indian sport called mallakhamb. The traditional sport sees gymnasts perform yoga positions while hoisted in the air on a wooden pole.

In the United States, pole dancing was derived from belly dancers called the 'Hoochie Coochie' or 'Kouta Kouta' dancers in the 1890s. Their embellished outfits, corsets and hypnotic moves caused a stir. By the 1920s, these movements were brought into circus performances by the very same Hoochie Coochie dancers, though in a more family-friendly way. Their athleticism and abilities were a sight to behold.

It was around the 1950s that pole dancing got its exotic flair, with clubs and bars installing poles, sparking the beginnings of burlesque and nude stripteases. The sexual revolution of the '60s only propelled this further.

The first recorded striptease was allegedly at the Mugwumps strip club in Oregon in 1968. A dancer known as Miss Belle Jangles, stripped while on the pole and it wasn't long before this idea took Canada, and effectively the Vancouver red-light district, by storm in the 1980s.

Stripteases were a sensation, not just because of the way they ended, but thanks to the seductive dances, costumes, themes and music.

Effectively, the modern-day strip club still hinges on a perfect mix of all these elements. Atlanta, Georgia is known to house the best strip clubs in the world, thanks to the popularity of Magic City, Pink Pony and Oasis. Offering some of the best food, DJs and entertainment in the city, these clubs all make bank thanks to one thing: butts.

Strong glutes are a prerequisite to achieving any of these outrageously difficult pole dancing moves, but the strip clubs in Atlanta take pole dancing to the next level by incorporating gravity defying twerking. (I dare you to Google old videos of Cardi B stripping.)

"YOU WANT TO HAVE A BUTT, THEN YOU HAVE A GUT."

Rihanna

Work It

CHAPTER 08

GLUTEUS HEALTH

You might not know it yet, but your ass is the key to your overall health.

Those buns of steel, whether they're droopy, bouncy or flat as a pancake, facilitate movements most able-bodied people take for granted. Climbing stairs, standing up, walking, crouching, twerking and everything in between are all thanks to our derriéres. Which means there are lots of benefits to keeping your booty happy.

Strengthening your back with the help of your butt

Experiencing back pain? Instead of focusing on the symptoms with painkillers and heating pads, target the source. It turns out that working on your glutes won't just alleviate any aches, but will also target the areas that need to be healed. Since your muscles hold your skeletal structure up, the way you work out can affect how you feel and the type – or absence – of pain one experiences. Strengthening your hips and booty can actually lead to a healthier lower back.

How? Your butt is actually made up of the gluteus maximus, medium and minimus. These are the muscles that allow you to move laterally, extend your hips, stabilise your pelvis and, more importantly, your back as you walk, run, dance and live your life. Exercise is key to not only protecting your hiney but improving its strength.

While you've probably heard of the gluteus maximus, since it is the largest muscle in your entire body, the other gluteus muscles are just as important to feeling strong. If the gluteus maximus is strong but the others remain weak, they'll have to overcompensate, which causes pain and injury. The gluteus medius is located on the outer surface of your pelvis and is responsible for stability and balance.

Here are three you can do right now – and don't forget to warm up.

The clam shell

As someone who struggles with exercise of any sort, the funnier the name a workout has, the more appealing it is. It's the kind of logic that won't get you far, but the clam shell is about to strengthen that ass and give your back the support it's been dreaming of. The clam shell exercise targets and helps to strengthen the gluteus medius, which can help to balance the pressure placed on your inner and outer thighs as well as your pelvic floor.

1. Lie on your side with your knees bent at a 45 degree angle, on top of one another.
2. Support your head with your hand.
3. Now, pull your belly button in to help stabilise your spine and pelvis.
4. While keeping your feet together, raise the upper knee as high as possible, but don't shift your hips or pelvis and don't move your lower leg off the floor.
5. Hold that position for a moment, then return your leg back to the starting position.
6. Find a pearl, put it in between your legs and call yourself a clam, because you just did it.

Repeat this 15 to 20 times and switch sides, repeating steps 1 to 6. If you want to turn the heat up on this one, add some resistance bands or a pilates ring.

Abduction glute bridge

Picture this: you're laying down on a comfortable yoga mat, arms are flat laying by your side and your knees are bent with your feet firmly planted on the floor. The next move is not only fun but going to give your back an extra layer of support that will more or less be life changing. Now all you need to do is thrust. Yes, you read that right. Thrust over and over again.

The abduction glute bridge doesn't sound as fun as the clam shell but it has all the charm. Just make sure that you keep your thighs lined up with the hip joints and add some resistance bands around your legs. Start with 10 to 12 movements and build that up slowly as you get stronger.

The best thing about this exercise is that it's deceptively simple and has a butt load of benefits. It targets the gluteus maximus and will help improve one's posture, strengthen the core, and tone and shape the bum, while helping eliminate lower back pain and even knee pain.

Squat with hip extension

Over the last decade, squats have become synonymous with toned asses, though their benefits aren't just physical. By using a resistance band and placing your feet hip-distance apart, the humble squat can be transformed into a move that strengthens the gluteus maximus and the back all in one. Hip extension moves are important because the hip extensor muscle facilitates your body's movements.

Working your ass off can help avoid gluteal amnesia

Gluteal amnesia may sound like the process of slowly forgetting all the joy butts bring to the world but it's actually when your body forgets how to activate muscles in your ass properly. The cause is sitting down too much. Whether you have a desk job, drive a car for a living, are an avid gamer, love watching television or just enjoy a nice leisurely sit down, the words 'gluteal amnesia' probably send a chill down your spine. You know what they say, use it or lose it! Luckily for all of us, it's fairly easy to fix.

Otherwise known as 'dead butt syndrome', this condition is the result of tight hip flexors which get shorter and more constricted the longer we sit down. The scariest part of this is that no one is immune to this condition, even those who work out regularly.

So what's the big deal about your butt getting amnesia? Well, when the glutes gradually lose strength, other muscles are forced to take on the load they no longer can, which can cause stress to other areas of the body. Knee pain, back problems and soreness in the hip can all indicate gluteal amnesia.

One way to test if your rump remembers how to do its job is to lie on the floor and place your hands under your butt. Once you're in position, try to squeeze your left butt cheek and then your right. If you can't feel your glutes engage then it looks like we need to jog your tush's memory.

The easiest way to reverse this is by standing tall and tucking your tailbone. Then flex your glutes as hard as you can for five seconds and release. Do this 10 times while waiting in line for coffee or washing the dishes, and you're on the road to recovery.

Adding a foam roller can help tremendously. Rolling out your hip flexors and the side of the leg can release something called myofascial tissue, which may be knotted and painful because of the lack of engagement.

Otherwise, try out the glute bridges and the clam shell discussed above and try donkey kicks, bird dogs and planks. Whatever you do, squeeze those cheeks like they've got the meaning of life wedged between them and don't let go.

The smell of farts can be therapeutic

Flatulence doesn't have the best reputation. However, a 2014 study by scientists at the University of Exeter revealed that tiny doses of hydrogen sulfides, a particle produced by the body when you let out a toot, can offer a range of health benefits. In fact, the study revealed it could be the key to the treatment of diabetes, strokes, heart attacks and dementia. That's not to say you should let off a few the next time you're at a hospital, but if you've ever been a little critical of a passing fart you might have missed the bigger picture.

Anal sex has its benefits, too

The body isn't just bound to oral, vaginal or clitoral pleasure. Turns out the butt is a hidden treasure trove ready for new sensations, intense orgasms and intimate experiences.

A 2010 survey by the *Journal of Sexual Medicine* found that amongst people with vaginas, 94 per cent achieved climax during their most recent anal sex session. Anal sex is becoming increasingly popular as stuffy residual stigma disappears and more sex-positive practices arise. More people are having – and being open about – anal sex than ever before.

"

MY APPRECIATION FOR MY BODY CAME ALONG WITH MY APPRECIATION OF JUST MYSELF IN GENERAL. WHEN YOU LEARN TO LOVE YOURSELF, AND KNOW THAT THERE'S NO ONE ELSE LIKE YOU, THEN YOU LOVE EVERYTHING THAT COMES WITH IT. YOUR FACE, YOUR BODY, YOUR FEATURES, YOUR CHARACTERISTICS, YOUR DREAMS.

Parris Goebel

"

CHAPTER 09

TAKE YOUR ASS OUT

Do you ever stop to appreciate all that your ass does for you in a day? You sit on it. You bundle it up in hot and sweaty conditions. Sometimes you even put it through the ordeal of public bathrooms. But no matter what, it pulls through every time. So maybe it's time you think about giving back a little and treating your derriére to some tender love and care.

Give your butt a spa day

Treating yourself to an at-home facial is as easy as buying a sheet mask and drinking a cup of tea. And leaving your butt as soft as a baby's bottom is just as simple. Booty facials now come in a diverse range of varieties, from $130 treatments at spas to DIY salves.

Since the skin on your ass is as prone to dryness, firmness and inflammation as your face, it pays to treat it well. The benefits are worth it too, whether you want to improve circulation, avoid acne or just generally promote healthier skin. Even though you can book yourself into a salon for the bumcial of your dreams, it's just as easy to achieve at home.

Time to exfoliate

First things first, try exfoliating your tush. Sugar scrubs are a great way to tackle sensitive areas, remove dead skin cells and leave your behind glowing. You can always buy one or put one together with stuff you already have at home. If you're looking for a store-bought solution, make sure that products are free from essential oils and fragrances, two things you definitely don't want to irritate you down there. Scrubs that include sea salt, sugar and jojoba oil are the way to go. As you probably know, using a scrub that includes crushed walnut shells on your face is a skincare sin, but the skin on your butt is far thicker and more resilient than your face. This means your butt and walnuts are a perfect match. There really is someone for everyone ...

The perfect DIY bum scrub

<u>Ingredients</u>

½ cup granulated sugar
¼ cup coffee grounds
¼ cup jojoba oil
1 tbsp coconut oil

<u>Method</u>

1. To make your DIY scrub, mix together the sugar, coffee grounds (a great way to reuse day-old grounds), jojoba oil and coconut oil and you're ready to go.
2. Once mixed together, bring it into the bathroom with you. Then scrub into your cheeks in a circular motion and wash off when you're done.

Butt masks exist, get used to it

Almost everyone has indulged in a face mask. Whether it's a
sheet, clay or peel-off option, they have the ability to make
your face glow while giving you 15–20 minutes of relaxation.
So the next time you slop on a mask, why don't you treat
your cheeks to a little luxury. Butt masks with sulfur or clay
will help absorb excess oils and build-up while fighting
inflammation and brightening the skin. Another holy grail
ingredient that your face and ass will both enjoy is hyaluronic
acid, which will keep the area looking hydrated and plump.
And if you're a little bit boujee (who isn't?), gold butt masks
do exist – they're even shaped to perfectly fit your peach.

Please come pH-correct

When it comes to giving your back end a good old rinse, there
are things you can do to keep it feeling fresh and healthy. Using
a pH-correct soap is the best way to do this. Your regular old
bar of soap tends to have a pretty high pH, that is much higher
than your skin, so keep those away from your anus. Body
washes fair a little better, but the kindest thing you can do is
to avoid harsh ingredients like sodium lauryl sulfate, sodium
laureth sulfate, synthetic colours and artificial fragrances.

Moisturising is essential

If spending too many hours on Reddit reading about skincare
has taught us anything it's that moisturising is essential. There
are a series of creams, salves and lotions on the market created
especially for your booty to keep it feeling supple. For solutions
with a firming effect, try something with a caffeine-rich
ingredient list, otherwise aloe vera, avocado and shea butter
are star ingredients to keep that bum looking and feeling good.

Massage those buns

The next step to pampering your buns is a massage, the kind that will leave you feeling soft, plump and rejuvenated. As we all know by now, our sedentary lifestyles aren't great for us – but did you know it's doing your behind a disservice too? Sitting all day weakens the glutes and hamstrings, and can lead to back pain. So whether you have a desk job or not, a massage can help immensely. Using a foam roller you can massage your butt by sitting on the roller, crossing your right ankle over the top of your left knee and then leaning into your right glute. Rolling back and forth, you'll start to get into those deep muscles that are screaming for some attention. Then you can do the exact same thing on the other side.

End the chafing

Two words: butt butter. For what it's worth, I realise that those two words probably mean something different on Urban Dictionary, but in actuality butt butter is going to save you from the dreaded effects of chafing. If you're hesitant to rub anything down there, as you should be, there are plenty of products out there to take care of your tush. Especially products made with beeswax, and other healing components such as aloe vera, calendula oil and, most importantly, arnica.

Oh my god, look at those bumps

Let's face it, our butts are as prone to acne, lumps and bumps as our faces are.

If you have buttne – butt acne – fear not, because there are plenty of solutions. Oftentimes breakouts on your behind are folliculitis, especially if they feel itchy or painful and appear as small, shallow bumps. To stop things getting worse, avoid scratching them. To prevent larger clusters you can try a few easy solutions.

Wash regularly with benzoyl peroxide, which will help prevent you from developing bacterial folliculitis. However, if it's caused by a fungal infection, an acne treatment just won't cut it. Using a dandruff shampoo to wash the area can help, but just make sure to leave it on for about 30 seconds before rinsing off.

If you have bumps on your butt that aren't acne, it could be keratosis pilaris. Keratosis pilaris is caused by follicles being blocked by dead skin cells and is commonly referred to as 'chicken skin'. It can give the appearance of goosebumps, though not to worry because it's totally treatable.

You may have heard of using acid exfoliants on your face, like lactic acid and salicylic acid, that can clear it up. Sadly, there isn't a cure for keratosis pilaris, but you can use an exfoliating scrub and cleanser, and creams with niacinamide to help smooth the texture on your bum.

Let your poop-shy bum sing

We really spent this entire book talking about butts but haven't even gotten to their function? As it turns out, asses are multifaceted, not only influencing history, but the entire music industry. Despite this, some people experience a very specific type of crippling embarrassment that renders them unable to poop in certain conditions. The technical term is parcopresis, which is otherwise known as psychogenic fecal retention. For people with parcopresis, taking a number two in a public restroom, at a friend's house or anywhere else that doesn't offer a certain level of privacy, is not just a cause of anxiety, but results in a physical inability to go. It may not currently be a medically recognised condition, but its effects are very real for a lot of people. While I'm not licensed in treating phobias, I do have a solution for those only mildly apprehensive about dropping the kids off at the pool (sorry).

If you're a little hesitant or are looking for ways to help friends feel a little less anxious about the whole ordeal, products on the market that eliminate odours can help. A mixture of essential oils traps odours under surfaces, so all you need to do is spritz before you go and never experience the embarrassment of opening the loo door again.

Keep in mind that caring about your butt isn't about achieving perfection. But it is about spending some extra time learning to love the most beautiful muscle in your body, one that helps you run faster, stand up tall and gives you a soft place to sit each and every day.

"

I LOVE MY BODY, AND I WOULD NEVER CHANGE ANYTHING ABOUT IT. I'M NOT ASKING YOU TO LIKE MY BODY. I'M JUST ASKING YOU TO LET ME BE ME.

"

"

WHAT MAKES
ME FEEL SEXY IS
BEING ABLE TO
ROCK NO MAKEUP
WHEREVER I GO.
ALSO, WEARING
PANTS THAT
SHOWCASE
MY BEAUTIFUL
ASSETS. IT'S MY
BUTT. I LOVE MY
BUTT.

Demi Lovato

"

CHAPTER 11

EMBARK ON YOUR OWN ASS-PIRATIONAL JOURNEY

As much as you might be aware of the way society works, it's hard not to get swept up in the hype. The ephemeral beauty standards that are forced on us can make even the most secure people question the validity of their bodies. You've had a butt since you were born, though many of us probably haven't really thought about it much until recently – and let's be honest, it's probably why you bought this book in the first place.

However you feel about your ass right now, take solace in knowing that it's all yours, incredibly unique and highly reliable. There's so much beauty in the small dimples littered across your cheeks and the curves that slope to give your derriére its unparalleled shape.

Learning to love your body is a cyclical process, one with peaks and valleys that may take you to places you've never been before. Whether that's learning about your ancestry that helps you to embrace your beautiful round behind, or discovering the genetics that give your small tush its spark, there is so much to be learnt about the bodies we're in.

They're passed down to us, by a long lineage of ancestors that we'll never meet but can be at home with just by looking down at our faces, hands, feet and ears, the bump on your nose or that curve in your back.

And for what it's worth, learning to love yourself in spite of trends that tell us we need a small ass one minute and a cartoonishly big one the next, is the ultimate win, is it not?

Time itself revealed a churlish history, one that went from exploitation of Black features to then commodifying them, while subsequently making anyone who doesnt fit into a certain mould feel bad for the sake of profits.

But together, we can change this. We can like – and even love – who we are in spite of the messages we're bombarded with and create a new chapter, one that recognises the pain of the past with the possibilities of a better future.

If you look around, these changes are already happening.

Most recently, Rihanna's Savage X Fenty runway show didn't just feature more Black models than ever seen in one New York Fashion Week show, but she also featured the late Mama Cax, an amputee and activist, on the same stage as Slick Woods, and Bella and Gigi Hadid. Laverne Cox strutted across the stage, while Aquaria did her thing, and Paloma Elsesser stunned, all choreographed by Parris Goebel.

It wasn't just a bombastic, multifaceted display of what women can be – powerful, sexual, pretty, happy, strong, fat, thin and talented – but a reminder that we aren't defined by any one thing.

That's a long way of saying that you are not your butt. And don't take anything I say as gospel, because I'm still figuring out my relationship with my own.

Sometimes I tense it in the hopes of avoiding gluteal amnesia and other times I forget it's there. I take belfies, shake it in the mirror, moisturise it and even give it a massage every blue moon. There are moments when I hate it, wish it were rounder, bigger or even softer, while other times I just wish it would fit into my favourite pair of pants again. But most of all, I'm learning to accept it. I'm going to celebrate my friends' butts when they wear a cute pair of jeans and I'm going to check one out every once in a while.

Butts are truly fantastic. So maybe it's time for you to set off on your own ass-pirational journey.

How?

Find the things you love about your tush. Is it a birthmark? Perhaps it's a perfect dimple or a funny tattoo you got a few years ago. Maybe it's the perfect size for a new skirt you bought, or the fact that it gets you tips when you dance at the club. It just might be because it's the perfect you-sized cushion wherever you need to sit down.

If you're finding it difficult to love it, why not take a belfie? Play with lighting, angles, themes and decor! Try dancing to a Big Freedia compilation of butt songs which will have you shimmying and sweating in no time.

Whatever you do, it's time to start giving yourself all the compliments, self-care and self-love you can, because your butt is worth it.

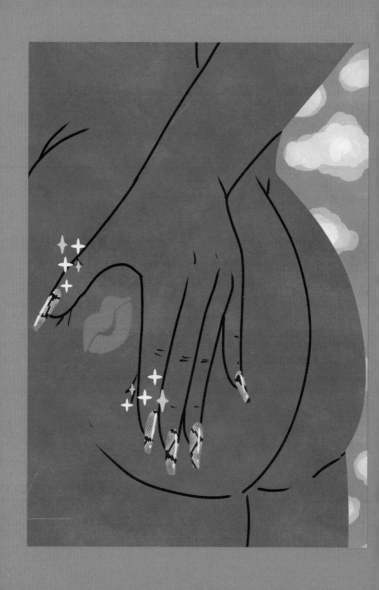